MIRANDA'S STORY

LUCY POSTGATE

GHP

Grosvenor House
Publishing Limited

This book is published by
Grosvenor House Publishing Ltd
Link House
140 The Broadway, Tolworth, Surrey, KT6 7HT.
www.grosvenorhousepublishing.co.uk

A CIP record for this book
is available from the British Library

ISBN 978-1-78623-986-0

Chapter One.

How to describe Miranda?

All the usual pony words would apply. She was exceptionally pretty. She was fast, feisty, and athletic. Most people would say she was cute and cuddly.

But Miranda would not have approved, for she was no ordinary pony.

She was hard-working, impatient and had no time for fools.

Miranda was bossy and demanded pony equality, even if it took her into a bit of a fight.

She was brave and would stand her ground.

When she brought up her own foal, it was with tough love. She was a devoted and protective mother, but there was no soppy nonsense.

If a pony can be called a feminist, Miranda ticked that box.

Miranda would have liked to have been a racehorse. She would have relished the fame and the glory. She would have been the fastest the world had ever seen, a flash of white light as she galloped past the winning post, fearsome and unbeatable. How she would have enjoyed leaving astonished geldings in a cloud of dust behind her.

Unfortunately, Miranda was only eleven hands and two inches high; a Welsh Mountain pony with tiny ears, dainty hooves and a fluffy coat so thick you could bury your hands in it.

She also had an incredible turn of speed and the courageous personality to go with it.

Miranda never gave up and she never gave in.

It was October 1996. Our children, George and Alanna, were nearly six and four years old. It was time to get another little pony so they could ride together. The days of one on Dylan, our elderly Welsh Mountain pony, and one in a push chair (or worse, in a back pack) were over. We needed two small ponies.

A friend advised me to visit a local Welsh Mountain pony breeder. Her farm was hidden down the winding, green, leafy lanes of East Sussex. It was a place you would never know existed unless you needed to go there, or otherwise found yourself there.

I made an appointment, explaining in advance what I was looking for.

The pony breeder said she had just the pony for me.

The pony was stabled and ready to meet me. He was sweet and well mannered, but apart from his wall eye, he was very ordinary. My heart didn't leap when I saw him. I was polite, as I did not want to offend the owner or pony, but I asked if I could possibly see some others before I made a decision.

We walked out into a massive field on the side of a hill occupied by Welsh ponies. Some came up to us, but most took no notice as we walked among them. There were ponies of all colours, from greys to chestnuts to bays and all the roan shades in between. There were blazes, socks, stripes and stars, all decorating perfect little ponies with dished faces. It was Welsh Mountain pony heaven.

The breeder pointed out the ponies she intended to keep and those which were for sale. There was too much choice – I would have liked to have taken them all home! Eventually, we came across a small mare. She was very dark grey, with a white face, black mane and tail, with white socks on her hind legs. She ignored us.

"Who is this?" I asked.

"Oh, that is Miranda," said the breeder, sounding a bit startled, as if she was surprised to see her there. "Yes, Miranda is for sale. She is five years old. We have not done anything with her apart from worm her and trim her hooves occasionally."

I rubbed Miranda's back and ran my hand down her legs.

"I will get her to trot for you," offered the breeder and promptly chased Miranda a few meters up the field, waving her arms.

Miranda trotted away - not far, before putting her head down to graze again. She refused to take any notice of us. I think she thought we were a bit batty.

I liked her attitude.

I departed from the stud very excited, having handed the breeder £50 deposit. I was much taken with Miranda's calm, independent outlook on life and I liked the prospect of training her all myself, rather than taking over where someone else had left off. Yet, she was five years old and therefore ready to be worked. Perfect!

Dylan was sure to be thrilled to have a girlfriend.

* * *

Get a Vet to look at your horse before you buy, I say to my clients. It's only sensible.

In my job as a riding teacher and horse carer, I am often asked to give advice on all kinds of horsey matters. Always happy to help, I say what I think is best. Interestingly, I have noticed people often go away and do exactly what they originally intended to do anyway.

I am no different. Two days later, without taking my own advice and consulting a Vet, George, Alanna and I took our trailer and the remaining £300 to collect Miranda.

She looked even smaller, darker and hairier in her stable than she had on the hill. She was like a furry toy, with two great big beautiful eyes.

Our new furry friend loaded into our trailer with no fuss and travelled beautifully. Miranda continued in her unflappable way, making herself right at home in our stable. She was far more interested in her hay than in us humans and only gave Dylan a passing glance.

I also received her passport at this time. Miranda was a rather posh Welsh Mountain pony. Her Dad was Symondsbury Skipper and Mum was Millhouse May-Bell, both greys. Her full name was Clipgate Miranda, though she quickly became Miri at our yard.

All went well overnight.

Whenever I arrived at the field, Dylan would greet me with a huge and excitable high pitch Welsh pony neigh. He was always very vocal. That first morning he had lots to say and was trotting up and down the field in high spirits. It was lovely to see Miranda's bearded face peering over the top of her stable door too. She could only just reach, so I made a mental note to get a bit taken off the top of the door for her.

The long term plan was for Dylan and Miranda to live out in the field together. Miri was unshod and Dylan only wore front shoes, so it was reasonably safe to put them out in the field together straight away. Without hind shoes, they would not hurt each other if they kicked out.

Dylan was not at all thrilled to have a girlfriend. He chased her away from her hay, nipped at her rump and stood in the gateway so she could not be petted by admirers. Miranda retaliated with half -hearted double barrelled kicks but was more or less unimpressed with Dylan's macho behaviour.

Later that day, I walked her from the yard to our house. This meant crossing the main A277. I had no idea how she would respond to the traffic, but I need not have worried. She was completely calm and much more interested in checking out our kitchen.

On day three, I put a saddle on her back.

Day four, she did some work on the lunge rein (a long rein used for the pony to move in a large circle around me) – only walking.

Day five, we progressed to trotting.

Day eight was her first flu and tetanus booster.

Day nine saw more lunging and a trip out in the trailer with Dylan.

By the end of the second week, Alanna was sitting up on her back.

We were up and away!

Chapter Two.

Dylan never admitted to being friends with Miranda, but he soon came to tolerate her company. So long as she knew her place in the field (several paces behind him) and always let him be fed first, he allowed her to stay.

During October and November, between the showers and gale force winds, the two ponies, George, Alanna and I went for many short walks. Dylan did not enjoy being on the lead rein. He had always preferred to walk just behind me, with his head in my back, but it was just too bad for him. I could already sense a little of the horse racing streak in Miranda, and I knew all about Dylan's competitive side, so the lead rein it was. It peeved them both – but kept my children safe.

Their competitive edge was useful in some ways.

In those days I rented a field known as The Croft, a mile away from my school. I had first rented The Croft when Dylan was a yearling. He had the whole six acres of permanent pasture to himself. The Winterbourne stream trickled through the field and he was sheltered by huge horse chestnut trees and old flint walls. It was a damn good substitute for a Welsh mountain, with banks and ditches and lots of other places for a small pony to hide. Dylan grew up fit and strong.

Over the following two decades (before the arrival of Miranda), the Croft diminished in size. The A27 became a dual carriageway, the Winterbourne stream went underground and the

Lewes by-pass was built. Nevertheless, it was still a great pony field.

In years gone past, I regularly walked Dylan along the main road to and from that field. Two ponies were going to prove more hazardous, plus the A27 was getting busier.

Through the winter Dylan only really worked in the riding school at weekends. It made sense for him and Miranda to spend the weekdays at The Croft. I decided to begin using the trailer to transport them, even though the field was only a short distance away.

In the horse world, we frequently hear about horses and ponies that dislike travelling, are difficult to load, and panic when they are enclosed, some of whom end up being downright dangerous when on the move. Others are only scared on the day of your important event, or even worse, suddenly take exception to your box or trailer when your important event is over and you are tired, hungry, need the loo and want to get home. There are horse people out there who earn their living training humans to train their horses to travel.

When my old mare, Gypsy, urgently needed X-rays, I travelled in the trailer with her to the Vet (this was in the days before the Vet could bring the X-ray machine to you). Tim, my husband, assured me he was only driving at 25mph, was really careful on the corners and used the brakes smoothly. It was still a most horrible experience being shut in an enclosed box with a large semi-terrified animal, who was struggling to keep her balance and not at all understanding why we were doing this. It was a seriously uncomfortable, sweaty, claustrophobic twenty minutes – and it *was* only twenty minutes! It is illegal to travel in the trailer with your horse, so don't try it at home, but I clearly understand why many horses take a dislike to travelling.

However, we had a job to do, and I needed to be able to the job by myself.

I organised the double trailer with the front breast bars across, and a manger with a few pony cubes clipped on to the far side of each breast bar. This little ploy meant that the ponies ended up with their heads over the breast bar – in the correct place.

Miranda and Dylan were quick learners. It became almost like a race to see who could get to their pony cubes most quickly. I just stood with them both at the bottom of the ramp, pointed them in the right direction and off they went. I quickly clipped on the back bars, shut the ramp, nipped round to tie their ropes and off we drove. When we arrived at The Croft, unloading was just as straightforward. They were also perfect ponies when the drive was done in the opposite direction – The Croft to the stables. I think they always felt something 'nice' was going to happen at the end of their journey. It is gratifying what a little food can do for a pair of fat, greedy, slightly combative Welsh Mountain ponies.

I was mighty proud of them both – particularly young Miranda.

Over the next few years, Miranda and Dylan accomplished the journey many happy times – always with enthusiasm. Eventually, modern life took over. The A27 just became too busy, the trip too time consuming and other drivers much less tolerant of a horse trailer and Landrover parked, even briefly, on the side of the road.

Reluctantly, I gave up The Croft. It is now a burger bar car park.

Chapter Three.

Miranda was a busy pony. Although Dylan was the 'boss', she was younger and much quicker than him. When he chased her away from her pile of haylage, she would whizz round behind him and eat his pile in no time.

At feeding times, Dylan would be waiting at his place by the gate. Miranda would always be somewhere else, checking something out, but would arrive at speed for her food.

When they were not living at The Croft, Miranda and Dylan lived in the paddock surrounding my outdoor school. I often let them have access to the school for extra playtime. In summer, it was a lovely dry, warm suntrap – ideal for a snooze. One sunny evening, I walked down the driveway to their paddock, only to be greeted by the sight of a smart red fox making off across the outdoor school with our black hen in its mouth. Before I had time to shout, there was Miranda, belting across the school in pursuit of the fox. The fox dropped the hen, who flew back to the stables with a mighty SQUAWWK! The fox disappeared over the fence and Miranda did a few celebratory bucks around the arena.

Was it just a coincidence? Or was Miranda really rescuing our hen?

Like riding schools all over the world, my school attracts a posse of enthusiastic teenage helpers – those girls and boys who will do loads of hard graft in return for a ride on a *pony*. Any pony will do

– big, small, slow, naughty, or exuberant, it matters not. A ride on a pony is worth many wet, windy Sundays' and hours of mucking out. I am all for child labour! I know exactly what it is like to be one of those teenagers, because I was one for years. How would riding schools manage without us?

With help from my posse, Miranda's riding school training began in much the same speedy and straightforward fashion as the trailer journeys. Ridden by my lightweight helpers, Miranda was soon able to tag along in lessons. It is a brilliant way to teach a pony – they learn a good deal by watching and copying their friends.

Right from the start, Miranda 'got it'. A classic novice lesson often begins with the leading file (front pony) trotting around the arena to the back of the ride. Miranda grasped this straight away and knew when it was her turn. I had barely uttered the 'M...' for 'Miranda's turn' and off she went – teenager mostly in control.

At first, it was quite funny and we marvelled at Miranda's intelligence and enthusiasm. As the months went on, she almost took over – anticipating what I was going to say before I had said anything. She was running my lessons – literally! I tried to speak in code to her riders and developed some subtle hand and arm gestures to tell the rider what was required next.

When I began to learn to teach riding in 1970's, our commands, the language we were allowed to use and the way lessons were conducted was very correct and regimented. A lesson would be given with military precision – sometimes not even referring to the pupils by name, but as a number. This was probably due to the long history of horses being used in the armed forces.

I remember being reprimanded more than once for asking a rider to 'catch up' in a lesson.

"Katchup is what you put on chips!" my instructor shouted at me.

I was supposed to say, "Second file, please close up".

We were also meant to take the lesson standing still in a corner, just off the track, with our hands held behind our backs. Definitely no walking around using arm gestures or standing with hands in pockets. It was quite hard – and often cold!

Happily, we are not so strict these days, but what one says and how it is said can be crucial.

Encouraging a youth to keep his horse active and energetic, I said, "Keep your legs on!"

"I usually do," he replied, looking down on me from his superior place high up on Ottie, my thoroughbred mare.

Or there is my favourite: "The whole ride, take your feet out of the stirrups and cross them over in front of the saddle."

I still have to be careful about that one when I am asking pupils to ride without their stirrups.

Occasionally, I put my voice training to good use outside of the riding school. I surpassed myself one day when our terrier pup, Griffin, was playing in the field with a fox cub. Instead of chasing the cub (which I thought terriers were supposed to do?), they were both having a wonderful game, running in and out of the hedgerow. First, Griffin would appear in the open field, panting, then the cub appeared catching his breath, and Griffin would disappear. Then, Griffin ran out and the cub hid. The game went on and on. It was enchanting.

However, they were beginning to get a bit near the main road, so I called Griffin back. He took no notice whatsoever. I followed them, calling, but the two continued their fun game of bouncing in and out of the bushes. By the time they were a few meters from the road, I was panicking. There was a split second when both fox cub and terrier were out in the open field. I raised my arm and pointed at Griffin.

"SIT!" I bellowed.

Griffin sat. And the fox cub sat too.

* * *

True to her Welsh Mountain breed, Miranda was extremely alert most of the time. She helped me to be very aware of how I conducted my riding school lessons, including the tone of my voice, my body language and even where I placed myself in the school (not necessarily on a corner, just inside the track).

Much later in her career at my riding school, Miranda gave me my only ever 'horse whispering' moment. In one of the fields we had a few little cross-country jumps. They were substantially made from ex-telegraph poles and basically built on the side of a hill, which was quite challenging for little people and ponies. Alanna was eleven years old and competent, riding Miri in a jumping lesson with other pupils.

There was one jump which became a big problem that day. It was a telegraph pole with car tyres hanging on it. The other ponies were jumping it easily from both directions. Not Miranda. She was sure there were bears, wolves and lions lurking within. Miri simply would not jump it.

We tried all sorts of tactics. I led her to the jump and let her have a good look from both sides. We asked her to follow another pony over it. We asked her to follow two ponies, but still could not persuade her. I parked myself and another pony either side of the jump as wings, but she still managed to get past the jump rather than over it.

It was exasperating and I could not really understand her fear. My daughter was becoming tired and sad for her pony. Miranda was dripping with sweat and anxious.

"Always end the lesson on a good note", says The Instructors' Handbook.

But how? I was at a loss as to what to do now. We were getting nowhere.

I walked up to Miranda and gave her a big hug. I rubbed her hot damp neck and whispered in her ear, "Just jump it, little Miri. Then we can all go home."

With a long collective sigh from the three of us, Alanna faced Miranda at the wolf-infested tyre jump one more time.

They popped over it perfectly.

I kept my word and we all went home.

Horse whispering? Nothing to it.

Chapter Four.

The turn of the century is worth a mention. After all, it only happens every thousand years. At school, the children filled a millennium capsule with memorabilia from the 20th century, including photos, small toys, artwork, a school book bag, school t-shirt and letters to future generations, which was then buried underneath a slab of concrete in the playground. Cricket pavilions, community centres, libraries, hospital wings, bridges and even a massive dome at Greenwich were built in honour of the third millennium. Impressive times indeed! We were optimistic and looked forward to the future.

Of course, there were the doom-mongers who said the 'millennium bug' would get us. The computers would crash. The clocks would stop and the world would end.

Mostly, though, people celebrated. The new millennium moved across the globe, beginning on the small islands in the South Pacific, then on to New Zealand and Australia, eventually arriving in the UK fourteen hours later. The fireworks began 'down under' with New Zealand and then Australia, who both put on huge and extraordinary displays. Families were glued to their television sets, as all over the world, countries seemed to be competing to put on the best show. Everybody was telephoning family and friends (Facebook did not appear for another four years) and parties seemed to go on for days. Even sleepy Lewes put on a firework display on the banks of the river Ouse on the Saturday.

At my riding school, it was more or less business as usual, except that Bug, my New Forest pony, had to be dressed up for the weekend as the 'Real Millennium Bug'. She took it all in her stride – an interesting change from the tinsel and antlers the ponies had worn at Christmas.

Normality eventually resumed. The computers had not crashed. The clocks had not stopped. Everyone above the age of three could spell the word 'millennium,' and no bug had affected our lives. People returned to their work and ordinary business. The world had not come to an end and the year 2000 got under way.

But, by far the most exciting event of the new century was yet to happen - Lobelia came to live with us.

I did not know Lobelia well before she came to stay, but I had seen her often enough, waiting patiently outside George and Alanna's school at the end of the school day. She was usually munching grass by the telephone box.

Lobelia lived on a farm in Kingston village, where she was a much loved member of a family. As is often the fate of Shetland ponies, her family had all outgrown her and Lobelia was looking for a new career.

Lobelia was kind and gentle with a reliable temperament. I knew this, because her owner admitted to sometimes leaving her youngest child in the care of Lobelia, while she herself nipped off to school to collect the others.

When I was asked if I would like Lobelia to come and live with us at Houndean, I jumped at the idea. Lobelia had a tendency to suffer laminitis, was a little wheezy, had sweet itch in the summer months, did not like whips and would not lunge.

But she could baby sit.

She was the pony for us.

Early morning, on Sunday 2nd April, Lobelia arrived with her chestnut coat, long flaxen mane and a whole trunk full of rugs and accessories. She was every small child's dream pony.

The bigger horses were horrified. There was much snorting and spooking and high blowing – what on earth was this thing? It moved like a pony. It smelled like a pony. It sort of made pony noises – but it could not be. It was far too small! What had happened to its legs? The horses ran to hide from Lobelia in the far corner of their stables, until curiosity overcame them and they had to take another look.

Only Miranda immediately saw a kindred spirit.

Another small, strong-willed, no-nonsense mare in the yard was perfect. Miranda and Lobelia became friends at once.

The one major difference between Miranda and Lobelia (apart from size and colour) was that Lobelia actually enjoyed being groomed, petted and dressed up. She also liked being washed and having her mane and tail shampooed. To Miranda, all these things were unnecessary, and as far as washing and shampooing were concerned, positively scary.

Miranda used to terrorise the children on the Saturday afternoon pony care sessions. All the children loved her and many were learning to ride on her, but the pony care was different.

Miranda was a good looking mare, now lighter grey than when she arrived, and just the right size to learn to tack up and groom. You would think she would be perfect for the job.

But Miranda had little patience with us. Being brushed was tolerable, as long as one got on with the job and was not apprehensive. If her groomer was nervous and stood as far away as possible, brushing with tiny, tickly strokes, Miranda would fidget and maybe tread on their foot.

If a child dithered and fumbled while picking out her hooves, Miranda would turn and give the child a quick nip. And there is nothing like the prospect of being nipped on the bum to make you dither and fumble.

Saddling up was no problem, but if the child made a hash of putting in the bridle, she would put her head up so high it was impossible to do. I think most people would agree that learning to bridle a pony is one of the most difficult tasks to master. Many times, I have seen beginners proudly fastening the throat lash and noseband. Standing back to admire their work, they find the snaffle bit dropped out of the pony's mouth some time ago.

On the plus side, Miranda did turn out some efficient pony carers. The pupils learned to help each other. One would hold Miranda's head (a skill in itself – stand to the side, not directly in front), while the other hoof picked. The bridle would eventually be mastered (usually practicing on Lobelia or Dylan first) and the sense of achievement was high.

With efficiency comes confidence. Those children that had been scared of Miranda on their first few pony care sessions were asking to do her – and to do her without help. As the pony carers became more proficient, so Miranda's behaviour improved. Until the next group of new pupils arrived, that is, and Miranda felt she had to boss them in to shape.

Miranda's ridden work in the school was going well. With Dylan and Lobelia in the small pony department as well, the lessons took on a new dynamic. We called them 'the small herd'. They were lots of fun. The year 2000 was looking good.

Chapter Five.

With both Dylan and Lobelia taking the little riders for lessons, a germ of an idea was running through my brain.

Should we breed a foal from Miranda?

Did I have room for another pony?

Would the foal have a home here for life?

Would it be fun?

It did not take long for me to decide that 'yes' was the answer to all those questions.

The riding school would always have a use for another Welsh Mountain pony. Dylan was approaching his 28th birthday, and there were subtle signs that he was beginning to age (not that I would have said that in his hearing!). There would come a time when he might want to take life easier.

There were plenty of riders at my school who would enjoy helping with the training of another youngster.

There was room at Houndean for another small one.

And yes - it would be fun!

A couple of foals had been born in these paddocks. Before I owned Gypsy, she gave birth here to Megan in the late 1970's. At much the same time, I stayed up all night at the neighbouring farm to watch Brunhilda arrive in the world, only for the mare to produce when I went home for breakfast. Bracken, a livery at the time, gave birth to Clover in May 1990. All these births were problem free, with the mares successfully producing in private without any help from us.

I had a little experience of foals and youngsters, but had never bred one of my own. It would be an adventure.

I made contact with the breeder from whom I had bought Miranda. She had several Welsh pony stallions. The one she recommended for Miranda was Rufus.

I went to meet him. He was a grey, section A Welsh Mountain pony, with a long flowing mane, a slightly dished face and impeccable manners. Section A Welsh ponies are the smallest of the breed – they stand under 12 hands 2 inches – so he would be perfect as a husband for Miranda. Also, as you may have gathered, I have a particular liking for small, grey Welsh Mountain ponies.

We agreed the Stud fee of £80 for the services of Rufus. The plan was that I would bring Miranda to stay at the Stud a few days before she was due in season. This gives the mare a little time to settle in. She would then be covered (horse term for mated) by Rufus when she was ready. Miri would then stay at the Stud for a month to make sure she did not come back in season. If she did not come back in season, we would assume she was in foal (horse term for pregnant).

I took Miranda off to meet Rufus at the end of May. We also booked a rare family holiday at this time. Lobelia could go back to her real owners in Kingston for a week or so and a good friend moved in to care for the other horses. It is quite a major event getting us away on holiday – seven assorted horses is not like asking someone to pop in and feed the cat.

The day before we were due to set off on our travels, I got a frantic telephone call from the Stud Manager.

"Miranda is kicking seven bales of shit out of Rufus!" she cried.

Oh my! I had not foreseen this. I did not expect Miranda to have an opinion.

"We can force her," she went on. "We can hobble her, so she cannot kick." She paused. "Or we can try a different stallion?"

Force her? Hobble my mare? Make Miranda have sex against her will?

There are some things that do not even need contemplating.

"I would like to try a different stallion, please," I said.

"Yes, that is, by far, the best way. Thank you. I will call you again tomorrow." The Stud Manager sounded relieved.

Very early the next morning, we loaded ourselves and our luggage into the Landrover and set off for our holiday. We were chugging our way down the M4 when I took the next call from the Stud.

"Good as gold," were the happy words. "Miranda took to Dick straight away. She has been successfully covered."

Phew! We might yet get a foal. No arranged marriages for Miranda. She had rejected Rufus and chosen Dick. She makes her own decisions.

We could get on with enjoying our holiday, and hoped Miranda was enjoying hers.

A mare's gestation period is usually between 330 and 345 days, or 11 to 12 months. Miranda was covered by Dick three times in early June. This would mean her foal would be due towards the end of May 2001.

Mares generally come in season every three weeks. Miranda did not come back in season, so I went to collect her in early July. I also thought I should meet this Dick chap she had chosen for herself.

Dick was a handsome strawberry roan stallion. He was bigger than Rufus, making him a section B Welsh Mountain pony. He sported the trade mark flowing mane and tail and dished face. He was a very striking chap – I could not fault her choice. I was not sure I was going to get my grey foal from him though, but you never can tell.

Later in the summer, the Stud had an Open Day. Alanna and I went to visit.

The first pony we came across was a little grey looking out over a stable door.

"That pony looks just like Miranda!" exclaimed Alanna.

"That is because she is Miranda's half-sister," said a helpful stable girl.

We were surprised by the clear family resemblance. I did not recall Megan looking very like Gypsy, or Clover being hugely similar to Bracken. Miranda and her half- sister could have been identical twins. There was much to learn.

The Stud was at its best. Who can resist a field of mares with foals at foot? There were real babies of only a few days old, foals of some weeks and big 'bruisers' who were several months old. It was a delightful place to be and made us even more excited for Miranda and her baby.

Chapter Six.

Miranda returned from the stud to join the small herd in the riding school again.

It was a summer when the sun shone, the sky was blue with scudding white clouds and the fields were dry. The small herd did lots of hacking out on the downs as well as work in the school. Our hacking here is spectacular. Riding on the downs above Houndean, the views stretch for miles. We can see the sea at Newhaven, the patchwork fields of the Sussex Weald and the green rolling hills of Firle and Kingston. Accompanied by birdsong and chirping grasshoppers, Alanna learned to take Lobelia out riding by herself - something she would not have been able to do with whizzy Miranda.

I did not sit on a pony until I was nearly ten years old. I admit to having been jealous.

Sometime in mid-September, it began to rain. We were pleased. It dampened the bone dry land and revived the grass and our vegetable garden.

Then, it rained some more. The rain became heavy. Then, it was a torrent. It was like having a bucket of water poured continuously over your head. The sky was no longer blue, but a really dark, menacing grey. The sun had gone - daytime did not get light.

The more delicate horses, Ottie, Gypsy and Killin (a Thoroughbred cross) began being stabled for the winter. This was a full two months earlier than usual, but the weather horses find most trying is rain and wind together. And we got it!

By October 9th, all the horses and ponies were living in stables or in their field shelters. Through the week the torrential rain continued, bringing with it thunder, lightning and strong winds. During the night of 11th and 12th October, fourteen inches of rain fell on Lewes Town and the surrounding area. This was equivalent to a month of rainfall all at once.

During the summer, Tim had converted some cattle pens into spacious loose boxes. The block was the height of luxury, brick built with a tiled roof and walls over which the horses could see one another and nuzzle each other, if they wanted to. That morning, I found my horses standing in water. It was extraordinary. The water had not come in through the doorways at the front, but through the back walls. I did not know water could travel through brick – I had assumed it would go around. Extreme water pressure, I am told.

A river flowed through the Houndean fields and a lake was beginning to form near the main road.

Miranda, who did not like getting wet anyway, was standing fetlock deep in water. Her grumpy expression said it all - "This is no way to keep a pregnant mare."

Problems for the people of Lewes Town were far worse than wet fetlocks. By lunchtime, the River Ouse had broken its banks. With a full moon due on Friday 13th and abnormally high tides, Lewes flooded. People lost their homes, businesses and their possessions. The RNLI were called in to help the emergency services. Only those living on higher ground escaped the devastation. I am writing this eighteen years on, but I can honestly say the horror of the flood and the massive clean-up operation is still vivid in the memories of Lewes' residents.

I did not see any of it. I spent the whole three terrible days at the farm mopping up wet ponies, wet bedding, wet rugs, wet children. I moved Miranda and Dylan back to the paddock round my outdoor school. The Winterbourne stream runs through this property. It is usually a gentle trickle and in the summer, disappears altogether. In October 2000, it was a ferocious torrent. I did not let the children near it. If they had been inquisitive and fallen in, they would have been swept away through the culvert tunnel and surely drowned. The Winterbourne lapped just inches from the top of its banks, but never quite managed to flood my stables or field. Miranda and Dylan kept their hooves dry.

It rained almost non-stop from September to April, usually accompanied by strong winds. Sometimes for a change, it was hail and then just before New Year, it was snow.

It was not just Lewes that suffered. The whole of the United Kingdom was battered, frozen and soaked.

As if the weather was not being harsh enough, February bought a major outbreak of foot and mouth disease in the UK. Foot and mouth disease affects cattle, pigs and sheep. Horses cannot catch it, but they can carry the disease. Our footpaths and bridleways were closed and the movement of all livestock was banned. My riding school could still operate, giving lessons in the school.

Farmers and their stock were not so lucky. It took from February to September to eradicate the dreadful disease. During those months, six million cattle, pigs and sheep were slaughtered across the country. The images on the television news and in the newspapers were of endless, enormous funeral pyres of dead animals.

Sometimes, it felt as if life would never be good again. We had long forgotten the optimism and hope at the beginning of last year.

Miranda stopped working in the riding school at this time. There was not much for her to do and her tummy was definitely expanding. As the spring slowly arrived, I changed her routine so that she lived in at night in the biggest stable. We called it the 'maternity wing'.

Even though the two mares which had foaled here previously had given birth in the paddocks, I was worried about Miranda. In the wild, mares tend to take themselves away from the herd to give birth. They then return when all is done and the foal is up and running. Miranda was such an independent soul, I just thought she might try and escape from the paddock to find a private place to foal. I had heard horror stories of mares damaging themselves by clambering over hedges, gates, or fences to give birth in solitude. Most mares foal at night. So that was Miranda's routine – out with Dylan, Lobelia and Gypsy during the day – then into the spacious maternity wing at night.

I had complete faith in a Welsh Mountain pony to deliver as nature intended. There was no CCTV. We did minimal late night checks. It was stress free.

On Saturday 26th May, we noticed milk on Miranda's teats. This is a sign that birth will happen shortly. Still, I felt no reason to change the routine in any way. Family life continued as usual with the cooking, eating and the washing up.

Tim took Griffin out for his late evening walk. Tim glanced in at Miranda before setting off. She looked like she was giving birth. He walked Griffin around the bridleway paths – a mere ten minutes. On his return, he peered into the stable again. There was another pony - a most delightful, beautiful, bay, filly foal.

Miranda had done everything in the best possible way. When I came down to the stable to greet them, Miri was standing up, her gorgeous baby at her feet.

It took a little while to persuade Miranda to let her foal suckle. We are told in every book - or these days, online - that the foal MUST take her mother's milk within the first hour. Tim, Alanna and I spent a frustrating time trying to persuade Miranda to let the foal take her milk. We pushed Miranda in a corner and pointed the baby in the direction of her teats. Miranda kicked and was not having any of it.

Well more than an hour later, we realised we were not helping and backed off.

We turned off the stable lights and waited outside.

Soon, in the quiet of the evening, we heard the very best sound. The foal was slurping greedily from Miranda's milk.

Miranda had it all organised. She did not need us there.

Looking back, and having had another foal born here more recently, I definitely recommend observing, but not getting involved unless really necessary. I think our presence, and probably some of our own anxiety, put Miranda off feeding her foal earlier.

Did I say bay? I did. Miranda did not give me the little grey pony that I had ordered.

The foal Miranda produced was not strictly bay either (although bay was the colour the Vet put on the foal's passport). I think one would call her a bay roan. She definitely had black points - black tips of the ears, muzzle, lower legs, mane and tail - but she also grew up with grey throughout her brown coat.

It became the trick question in the riding school. "What colour is Miranda's daughter?"

Over the years, the foal also had dapples, spots, white eyebrows and zebra legs. She was always interesting, often more grey than bay, and we agreed that she changed colour with the seasons.

The question should have been, "What colour is Miranda's daughter today?"

Naming the foal was always going to be tricky. No, you cannot call her Bambi just because she looks like Bambi. Hopefully, she would grow into a pony, not a Disney deer. Nor can she be Michael (Jordan). I had to be quite firm about this with my children.

It took a week of passing prospective names about – mostly beginning with 'M', as I wanted to continue the May-Bell/Miranda theme from the stud. We eventually plumped for Mia, or Houndean Mia, to be precise. The name 'Mia' has Latin origins meaning 'mine', or 'much wished for child', which seemed to fit nicely.

Miranda was an excellent mum. She made plenty of milk and allowed Mia to suckle whenever she wished. Miranda was besotted with her baby, but not overly so. She allowed us to handle Mia right from the beginning. To get them out to the paddock by day, it worked best to push the foal rather than lead her. We then progressed to pushing at the same time as leading with a soft scarf around Mia's neck. We then got on to the foal slip, scarf and pushing, eventually dispensing first with pushing and then the scarf.

You would expect Mia to follow Miranda wherever she went, but this was not always the case. Mia was inquisitive and did not necessarily want to go back into the stable at night. Miranda would be in the stable tucking into her supper.

Mia would be planted in the doorway watching everything else that was going on, refusing to budge. Luckily, she was tiny and I could more or less lift her up the step and carry her in.

Miranda had a year off work just being a mum. She and Mia lived together in the same stable or field until January, when I decided to begin the weaning process. It is easy to wean here, as the ponies can see each other over the stable walls, but Mia would not be able to take milk. Miranda's milk would take a week or two to dry up. Of course, they were not happy about being separated, but it seems to me to be a less distressing way of weaning than taking one of them away completely and shutting the other in a dark stable so they cannot jump out. We did the same in the field during the day, with a good flint wall in between them.

It worked well. Within a month, they were both out in the field together with the small herd – fewer responsibilities for Miranda and plenty of playmates for Mia. Better times had arrived with Mia.

Chapter Seven.

Some horse people say, if you let a mare have a foal, it will calm her down and give her a reason to chill. Hah! Not our Miri.

Miranda returned to riding school work full of enthusiasm, raring to go and ready to take over my lessons again. Mia came down to the school too. She quickly got used to watching her Mum work and there were usually people around who wanted to groom and pamper her. In later life, if Mia did get anxious about anything, a good way to persuade her to relax was to brush and plait her tail.

* * *

If there is one aspect of riding about which I am really fussy, it is getting the rider's balance and seat good. If you learn to ride with an independent, balanced seat, you and your horse will be comfortable and safe. You will have no need to hold on for dear life. If you are not prepared to put in the groundwork to get this right, best not to get up on one in the first place.

I have lost count of the number of times I have been at a social gathering/party/school event when some man (sorry, but it nearly always is a man) says, "I hear you ride horses?"

Short pause. I know what is coming.

"I can ride a horse. I galloped Arabs all around the Pyramids/the Gobi Desert/Lapland. Fantastic! I could not sit down for a week. My knees were bloodied and my hands were torn. It didn't do much for my sex life either. Haw! Haw! Marvellous fun though. Gosh, I can ride those things."

Cringe-worthy.

Am I supposed to congratulate this person? All I can think of is the horse. How did the horse cope with an incompetent tourist bumping about on its back for hours?

Not every social encounter is like this. Sometimes it is just, "I hear you ride horses? I rode a horse once. It threw me straight off. I'm scared of them now."

At least with that conversation, I feel the horse was probably uninjured and was allowed to go back to the stable.

What I really want to reply to these people is, "Get lessons. Get taught to ride properly."

But I don't. Instead, I smile politely, knowing the case is hopeless.

'Klingons' to most people are the extra-terrestrial, baddie warriors in Star Trek. There is quite a cult of 'Klingon' lovers at present.

What you don't know is about is the other 'cling-ons'.

To Miranda, 'cling-ons' are riders who get on her back, tighten the reins so short her mouth hurts, then clamp their legs on her sides, while leaning forward in galloping position. The 'cling-on' on Miranda is usually tense, holding its breath and giving off all sorts of terrible vibes. Miranda hates them. They are more frightening to her than anything from outer space.

Being small, Miranda had to teach many beginners. These were never a problem, as the lunge rein is a good place to start, holding the saddle and doing simple exercises to get that coveted 'good seat'. Miranda was happy with this.

The 'cling-ons' were usually children who had ridden elsewhere, but probably had not had lessons, or kids who had their own pony but no lessons and had learned to stay on the pony any which way they could. Once the rider was mounted and got his or herself into clinging on position, Miranda would shoot off, because in effect, that is what the child was telling her to do. It always ended in disaster. If you hold on to something too tightly or for too long, you eventually let go. And if you happen to be on a fast pony, you will fall off.

As a riding school, I have to keep an Accident Book. When I was a child, we fell off all the time. It was like a badge of honour. We used to compare bruises.

In this risk averse 21st Century, any fall from a pony is considered an 'accident' and has to be recorded and signed by me and the parent or pupil. To make it a bit more light-hearted, we keep a Horse Scores Chart. Each time someone falls off, the pony or horse scores a point. The points are counted up at the end of the year. Miranda always won.

I remember one keen young girl who began riding with me, having lessons on Lobelia. Lobelia could be really quite naughty. Sometimes, for apparently no good reason, she would suddenly turn 180 degrees and end up facing the pony behind. This always caused chaos, because whichever horse she happened to face would be horrified and stop dead. Lobelia also loved to canter with her nose nearly on the ground and was famous for her baby rears. Rearing is a serious problem, but Lobelia merely lifted her front legs a few inches off the ground, so was not in the slightest bit dangerous or frightening. She once saw off a stray goat by doing her baby rear. She was never in trouble, because she was so small and cute and funny.

Everyone who begins riding on Lobelia has to move on to Miranda at some point. The young girl I am thinking of got to that point. Her balance was good and she was getting a bit long in the leg for Lobelia. In truth, I don't think the girl was nervous at first, but the mother was.

Each week the mother would come to me before the lesson got underway and say, "Fenella is a bit nervous today." (She was not called Fenella, but I will use that name).

Every week, the girl would turn up with the mother, looking more apprehensive.

"Fenella is a bit wobbly today."

Some of you will have guessed where this is going. The day came when both mother and daughter arrived visibly shaking.

"Fenella is rather worried today."

Fenella mounted Miranda. She was trembling and instantly got herself into classic 'cling-on' position. Miranda took off – with terror. Ponies feel fear and there was a lot of it about.

I cannot remember if Fenella fell off, or if I somehow persuaded Miranda to stop. Certainly, the child's riding career was over. The thing that parent and child had feared so much had happened.

I felt sad for everyone, including my pony. The girl obviously wanted to ride, or she would not have turned up at all. I often wonder if I should not have let the child get on Miranda that day. Maybe I should have recognised the real fear in mother and daughter? There is nervousness because you know riding holds some risk, but you want to do it anyway. And there is real fear. My instinct is to encourage my pupils to continue and hopefully conquer the fear. I want them to enjoy the sport as I do. Sometimes it just is not going to happen. It is a hard call.

There was another girl who rode Miranda, who got herself into such a fearful state that she would not get out of the car when she arrived for her lesson. She stopped riding for a whole year. When she returned, she became one of the best, most sensitive riders this school has turned out.

All this makes Miranda sound as if she should not be in a riding school. Not so. She was a great teacher and very popular. The pupils who mastered the art of sitting comfortably and giving clear, gentle aids had a fabulous time on her.

We had a party for Dylan's 30th birthday. Miranda won nearly all the races. Yes, she cheated a bit and created a few false starts, but she was the pony everybody wanted to ride. Little and quick beats a fifteen hand horse every time.

She was also a keen jumper (as long as the jump was not wolf-infested), winning many rosettes for her riders, both at my school and elsewhere.

I think the only dent in her ego came one day when we took Bug and Miranda to a big local show. There were loads of classes and all sorts of experienced ponies and riders doing clever things. Miranda was in 'family pony' and behaving very well. Alanna and Miri did a good show – maybe a tad fast. They were placed last in line as the rosettes were given out.

The lady judge looked down at them. "She is not really a family pony, is she?"

How rude! Miranda IS family.

Chapter Eight.

Very sadly, the autumn after Mia was born, I had to have Gypsy put to sleep. She was thirty three years old. She had had a tremendous life and a grand summer with Miranda and baby Mia. Arthritis had been giving her problems for a while. One day, in spite of her daily dose of anti-inflammatory drugs, she just did not want to make that small step down out of her stable door. I realised the time had come. It was the first time I had had to make that decision in cold blood, as it were. With the Vet, I led her to our meadow. She was a little sedated and I worried briefly that we were not going to get to the right patch in time, but we did. The Vet gave her the lethal injection. It was humane and calm. With a machine, Tim dug a huge pit and buried our old mare. I did not watch this bit, but sometime after I had to know, "How did she go in?"

"Curled up like a dormouse," he replied.

* * *

Life in the riding school went on. We were joined by a glamourous five-year-old American Quarter Horse. She was dark bay, with a star and stripe (naturally), nearly fifteen hands and called Kir Royale. Wow!

Miranda was not sure about this. The newcomer presented some serious competition in the speed stakes. There was a period when I regularly took two adults out hacking on Kir Royale and Miranda.

Every time we went out, there was an unexpected race. All I would see from my sedate canter on Killin was the sight of Kir Royale and Miranda's rear ends disappearing across the landscape. Exasperating! I had to apologise to walkers as I rode by.

"Hooligans in all walks of life," commented one hiker.

Mia joined the work force. Like her mother, she was a quick learner. She was also a slightly calmer personality and incredibly comfortable. It was almost difficult to teach a beginner rising trot on Mia, because sitting trot was so easy. Perfect for getting that much sought after balanced seat, though.

Mia never loved jumping like her mother. Miranda's jumping career was really taking off. She was almost a 'point and shoot' pony - point her at the jump and she would go! If the rider's steering was slightly inaccurate, Miri would soar over the wrong jump. She also perfected a nifty STOP on the landing side if the rider had lost balance. That bumped up her Horse Score points nicely. It was good having Miri and Mia in the same lesson. They worked well together.

When I went to view a part-bred Welsh Cob with the possibility of buying him, I took Alanna and her friend with me.

"Ooh! He looks just like a big Miranda. We MUST buy him!" they said.

So we did.

Lynbrie Storm did look like Miranda. He was white grey with big eyes, a bit of pink on his muzzle and an admirably muscular physique. That is where the similarities ended. He was not brave – he was scared of most things. He was not fast and feisty – he was a lazy cob preferring a quiet life. To be fair, he was a talented jumper, which surprised us, although he would never have won a speed competition.

Storm went to live in the same field as Miranda, Mia, Bug and Tippy (Kir Royale had become known as Tippy). That first summer, they ended up being called 'the Fearsome Five'. No one pony was particularly fearsome, but the combination could be quite hair-raising. Storm thought he had landed in paradise, living with four beautiful mares. Bug fell in love with him. Tippy thought he was pretty cool too. Miranda thought his presence was an affront. Mia stayed safe behind her mother.

Normal grazing was fine. Difficulties only occurred at catching up time. They all wanted to come in at the same time and Miranda particularly had it in for Storm if he got too close to her. She would fly at him with her ears back, then gallop away because she was not stupid and realised he was four times her size and strength. Sometimes, there would be four of the fearsome five bucking and kicking round the gateway – all trying to be scary, but also keeping out of the way of each other. One memorable time, I was holding Storm and Bug in their headcollars, waiting to take them out of the gate, when Miranda flew at them. She missed and knocked me over instead, leaving her muddy hoof prints up my back. I was not hurt, because the mud was deep and soft. Not a pretty sight, though.

In the riding school behaviour was much better. Storm and Miranda, the little and large lookalikes, performing a double ride together was a joy to watch.

Hacking out with the two of them was also lovely. Storm had no wish to enter into a race with Miranda. When she was revving up, hoping for a bit of competition, he would merely bounce into canter for a few strides and then take it easy. It was pleasantly peaceful.

Chapter Nine.

Towards the end of 2013, there were warning signs that all was not going so well for Miranda. At first, there was nothing to cause alarm.

She would come in from the field extra dirty, appearing to have made a big effort to cover herself all over with mud, including her face.

Her appetite was good and she was always ready for her feed, although she was not as well covered with fat as I would have wished.

Occasionally, even with a rug, she was shivering in the early morning.

I decided to keep her stabled at night. This was something she would have hated in her youth, but now, at the age of twenty-two, she seemed to appreciate.

Miranda was still enthusiastic at work and also happy to go out in the field daily.

One day I had to call the Vet, because Mia had a swollen, sore eye. As I waited for the Vet, in the next door stable, Miranda went down to roll. How cute, I thought, until I realised that this was not a healthy happy roll, but a tummy ache roll. When the Vet arrived, I had to explain that he was now treating two ponies. Good timing. He prescribed eye drops for Mia, something to settle Miranda's guts and pain relief for both. Within hours, mother and daughter were much improved.

Later in the winter, there was an unpleasant incident in the school. Miranda was being ridden by a good little rider who adored her. We had a jumping course set up. The pair jumped the first and second. At the third fence, Miranda, our super show jumper, failed to take off. The rider was thrown clear, though was unhurt. Miri did a complete flip over, a truly horrible sight to see. She got up from the ground quickly, trembling, unhappy and sore.

Some days later, she did the excessively muddy rolling trick in the field again, coming in absolutely plastered in mud.

A few days after that, she had another minor colic.

This did ring alarm bells, but the colic was over as quickly as it had begun. Then, she would perk up and be hungry again.

I varied Miranda's diet a bit to see if I could pinpoint a problem. My horses and ponies are fed exclusively on lucerne pellets (which are high in calcium and act as an acid buffer) and timothy haylage – both feeds being gentle on the guts. I bought Miranda an aromatic mint feed supplement. I was not convinced that the feed was causing her colic.

Her back was becoming noticeably more dipped, which was odd. I had my chiropractor to treat her regularly and a saddler advised me to use a special pad under her saddle.

When she had her annual boosters and dentistry done, I discussed my concerns with the Vet. Her temperature, pulse and respiration were normal. Her coat was glossy and she was still eating well. Her gut noises were as they should be.

As the summer and warmer weather arrived, she went to live full time in the field again. Storm had become some kind of bullying thug and was banned from living with the mares (see his own book). Even without him in the field, Miranda managed to get herself kicked in the ribs.

This was the moment I finally grasped that something was very wrong. Miranda would never have been kicked in the past. She was far too quick and had never lost a fight.

I kept her separate from the others now, letting her graze alone or with Mia only.

* * *

Our other terrier, Boo, is very barky. She barks in the night if a fox or badger dares to venture onto her patch. She howls like a wolf if there is a squirrel outside and she cannot get at it. She has a short sharp bark if she has chased that squirrel up a tree. She has a woofing bark to announce the arrival of strangers and a low menacing growl for snakes. She has a special high pitch bark for a cornered rat. It is unmistakable.

One morning, I rode back from a lesson in the outdoor school. Miranda was grazing alone in the field we call the football pitch. I untacked and went on with my chores. Boo was barking. Not unusual, so I took little notice. Only this barking went on. It was not a bark I had heard before. It was different.

I called Boo. She did not come to call and continued to bark intermittently. It was a call for help.

Boo was standing guard over Miranda, who was lying down, filthy with mud and very ill. All those excessive mud rolling days had not been fun. She had been in pain.

The Vet came quickly and diagnosed colic. No surprise there. With the help of the Vet, Miranda recovered quickly as she had done before. By 9.30 pm, she was slurping a warm feed of lucerne and mint.

Early next morning, Miranda was upright and neighed when she saw me. I felt momentary relief until I looked in at her. One glance filled me with dread. She was sweaty, shivering and had passed very few droppings.

We rushed her to the veterinary hospital as an emergency. The Vets set to work at once with pain relief, blood counts, an ultrasound scan of her intestines and a belly tap, which drew a sample of fluid from her abdomen.

All the results were as bad as they could be. The Vets were astonished that Miranda had come this far with so much wrong inside and so little complaint. What an amazing, stoic, brave little mare.

I held her close to me as she was put to sleep.

It was a complete shock. I could not believe this was the end. Her original sparring partner, Dylan, had lived until he was thirty eight.

Our beautiful, courageous Miranda was gone from us far too soon.

* * *

Mia was a sad pony. For such a long time, she watched for her mother, waiting for her to come back. Even now, years on, if she sees a little grey pony in the distance, she gazes for longer than she should.

Mia took on all the small riders who had learned on Miranda. She became a perfect angel in the school, being much more tolerant than her mother. She never won the Horse Scores. She liked people. She was kind to the other horses, even letting our newest arrival, Scout, share her food in the field. Much to his surprise, she made Storm her friend, so long as there was a good stone wall between them both.

Miranda lives on in her gentle, peaceable, almost bay coloured daughter.

* * *

Mia is seventeen now and a responsible grown-up.

Very occasionally, something strange happens.

Without warning, and quite out of character, Mia will take off round the field at a gallop, adding in leaps and bucks as she goes. She is flying like a Pegasus, her hooves barely touching the ground.

Is Miranda galloping alongside her, the spirits of thousands of years of Welsh Mountain ponies in their wake – racing to keep up?

About the author

Lucy Postgate's horse riding career began as a young child playing ponies cantering around her London bedroom. After the family moved to East Sussex Lucy began to learn to ride real ponies at Hope in the Valley Riding School in Lewes. She was aged ten. Lucy went on to take and pass her BHSAI in 1975 and has been running her own riding school since 1977. Lucy is married to Tim Duffield. They have two grown up children, George and Alanna.